THE
POSITIVITY
COLORING BOOK

THE
POSITIVITY
COLORING BOOK

*Brighten up your day
with these joyous images*

SIRIUS

This edition published in 2024 by Sirius Publishing, a division of
Arcturus Publishing Limited,
26/27 Bickels Yard, 151–153 Bermondsey Street,
London SE1 3HA

ISBN: 978-1-3988-4475-9
CH011803NT

Printed in China

INTRODUCTION

Your outlook on life can be crucial to how you feel and how you perceive the world around you—whether as essentially friendly—or as hostile and unwelcoming. Trying to take a positive view can help to actually make your experiences more upbeat and fulfilling. The images in this coloring book aim to generate a sense of positivity, both through what they are depicting and the process of coloring them in. You'll find pictures of cheerful animals, sunny landscapes, and relaxing pursuits like sailing, as well as delightful experiences such as stroking a cat, a country walk, or gardening. Take a deep breath, carve out a couple of hours in your busy day, make a selection of your favorite colored pens or pencils, choose an image, and begin to create a sense of positivity through your coloring.

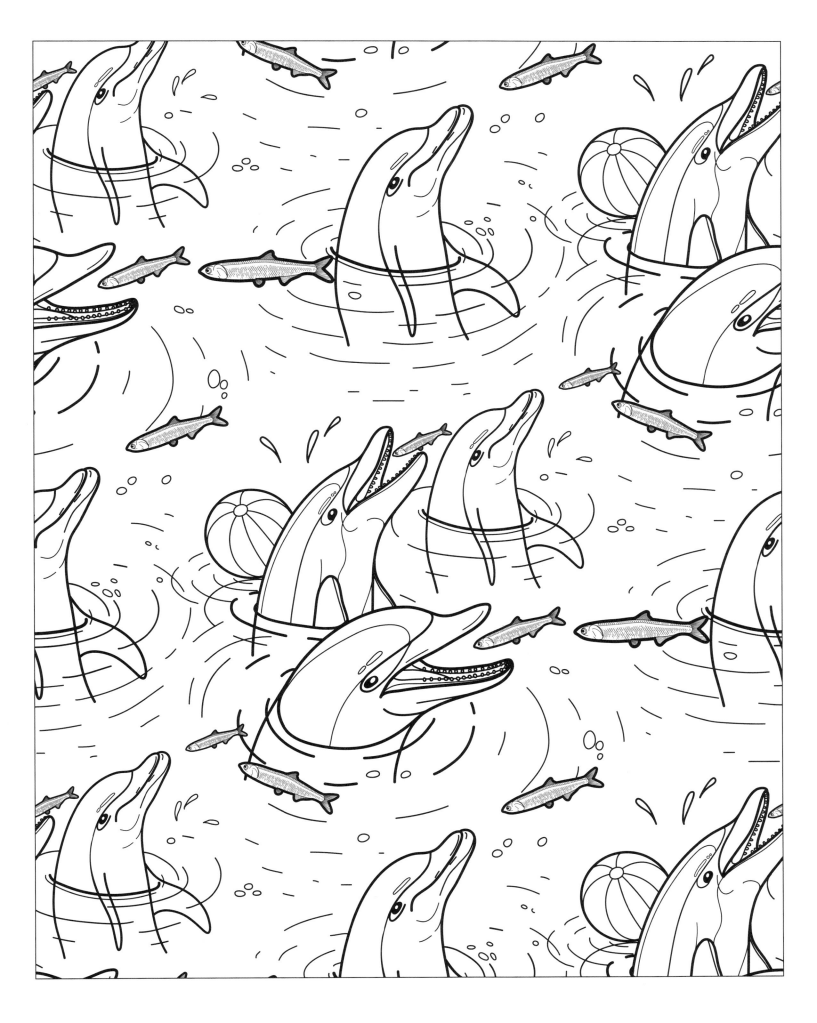

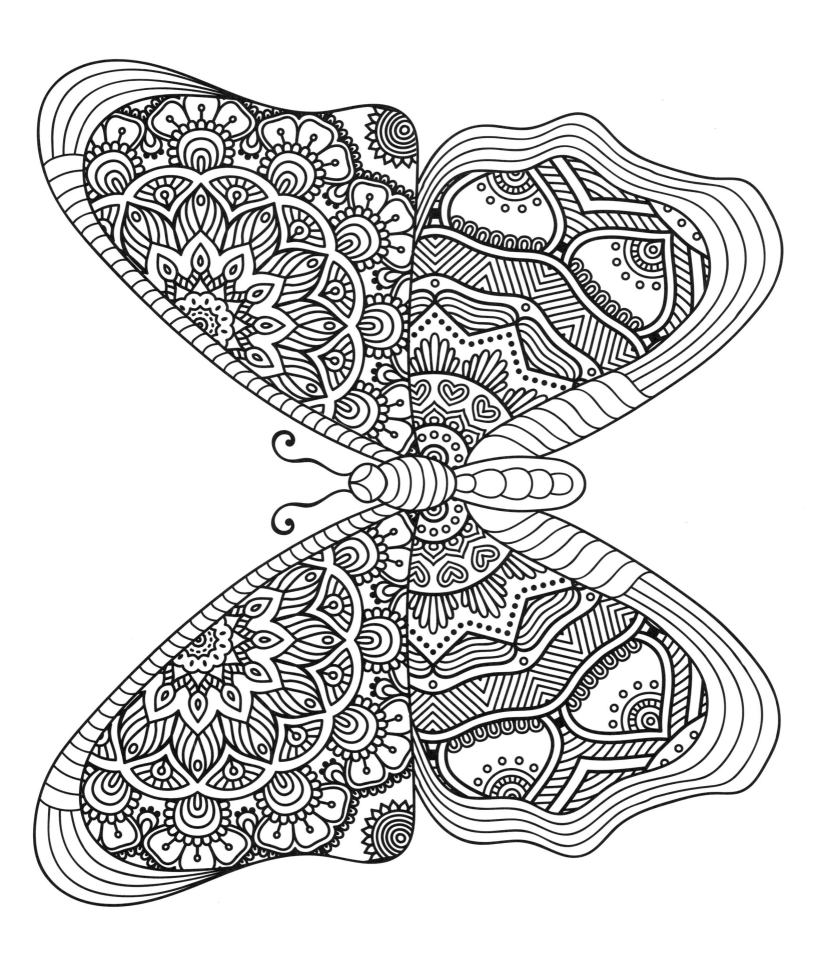